Mary Had A Little Lamb

by
Susan Panzica

Illustrated by
Zach Brose

Mary Had A Little Lamb
Published by Eternity Cafe Publishing

ISBN 13: 978-0692525906
ISBN-10: 0692525904

Copyright ©2015 by Susan Allen Panzica

Illustrations ©2015 by Zach Brose

Library of Congress Cataloging-in-Publication Data
Panzica, Susan Allen.
Mary Had A Little Lamb / by Susan Allen Panzica; illustrated by Zach Brose.- 1st ed.
p. cm.
Summary: The story of Jesus' birth with timeless life lessons.
ISBN-13 978-0692525906
[1. Christmas – Nonfiction. 2. Christian life – Nonfiction. 3. Children– Non fiction]
I. Brose, Zach., ill. II Title.

Printed in the United States of America
First printing, 2015

Dedicated to:

Lauren and AJ, my ever brilliant sources of inspiration
and
Tony, who taught me you're never too old to rock and roll,
or dream a new dream,
or write a book.

Without these three loves of mine, this book wouldn't exist,
and my life would be so much less.

Mary had a little Lamb.
His name was Jesus Christ.
He came to save this world of ours
and give eternal life.

He had a home in heaven
before the world began.
He left His throne and glory
to become just like a man.

He said unto His Father,
"I'll go to do Your will,
It might not be what I want,
but I will do it still.

And so His home He left behind
and came to us on earth,
filled with love for people
who would marvel at His birth.

Mary and Joseph heard from God
when an angel had appeared.
He told them not to be afraid -
with God, there is no fear.

The angel spoke to Mary,
then to Joseph in a dream.
Said they'd have the Son of God –
How shocking it did seem!

They traveled far to Bethlehem
for that was Joseph's home.
They couldn't find a place to stay.
They felt tired and alone.

God led them to a humble place
where the Child would be born.
A moment that would change the world
we call it Christmas morn!

It was not a royal palace.
It was not a rich man's home.
It was just a lowly stable
in which animals did roam.

Shepherds out in the fields that night
tended to their flock.
An angel of the Lord appeared.
They filled with fear and shock!

"Do not be afraid," he said,
"I bring good news and joy!
In Bethlehem, a Savior's born—
a swaddled baby boy."

More angels soon appeared to them
with praises greater still,
"Glory to God in the highest,
and on earth, peace and good will."

And so they ran to Bethlehem
and saw the Babe so small.
They gazed in adoration,
and then spread the news to all.

Later came the wise men
who traveled from afar.
They fixed their gaze on heaven,
being guided by a star.

Precious gifts of gold and myrrh
for the Child they did bring.
They bowed down, full of joy,
and worshipped Christ the King.

The baby's name was Jesus
which means that He will save
God's people from their sins,
and He'd teach them to behave.

He grew up wise and mighty
with power from above
doing many miracles
showing His great love.

But then He hung upon a cross,
a crown of thorns upon his head.
He died to take away our sins
and save us like He'd said.

Then tears gave way to smiles
when the stone was rolled away.
He triumphed over sin and death–
We call it Easter day!

And now, He sits in heaven
upon His royal throne,
His Holy Spirit speaking
to those He calls His own.

To any who receive Him
He gives amazing grace—
to be called a child of God
and someday see His face.

Now you can be a shepherd
and share the greatest news.
As His child, you can be
someone God can use.

You can be a wise man,
down on bended knee
giving gifts of worship
and showing generosity.

You can be just like them
traveling far or near
telling of God's greatness
to any who will hear.

For God did speak to Mary

and He spoke to Joseph, too.

And if you listen with your heart

God will speak to you!

Dear Parent,

I wrote this poem for my children to provide a deeper picture of what Christmas is really about - the whole life of Jesus and the reason He came to us. I wanted them to move beyond thinking of Jesus' birth as a sweet story about a baby in a manger and know it as a part of Scripture every bit as significant as the rest, bringing essential life messages, most importantly, that God is real and speaks to us and to them today.

This book is not meant to re-tell a familiar tale. Please allow the words in these pages to impart life lessons that will last long after the wrapping paper is discarded and the ornaments are put away.

As you read this book, I challenge you to set aside the familiar and look with a fresh perspective. Here are some talking points to share with your children that may speak to you as well. And then, let's look at some myths, familiar assumptions NOT in the story and separate fact from fiction.

Talking Points

Mary Had A Little Lamb challenges us to look past the familiar and often false beliefs about the Christmas tale, and let it take on a deeper meaning for you and your family. Too often, the whirlwind called "the Christmas season," filled with traditions of fiction and fantasy, overshadows the facts that are the foundation for the festivities.

Here are some observations and questions to discuss with your children and provide greater insight into the well-known story.

And don't hesitate to open the Bible for yourself, and let God speak to you!

Mary had a little Lamb.
His name was Jesus Christ.
He came to save this world from sin
and give us eternal life.

Is "Christ" Jesus's last name?
No, it is His title. Christ is from the Greek word "Christos" meaning "Anointed One" or "Chosen One" and is the equivalent of the Hebrew word for Messiah: "Mashiasch."

And He had a specific purpose in coming to earth: "... *to seek and save the lost.*" (Luke 19:10)

God has a special purpose for you too.

When did Jesus' life begin?
Read Col. 1:15-23. In verse 17, we read that Jesus "*existed before any-thing else.*" His life did not begin when He was born on earth. He simply changed geography by joining people on earth.

Jesus was alive before His life on earth. And He lives today! Eternity has no beginning or end.

Did Jesus feel uneasy about leaving heaven to come to earth, to enter Mary's womb, and be born to live and die like a man?
Before Jesus died, He prayed: "*Father, if you are willing, take this cup from Me; yet not My will, but Yours be done.*" When He said "cup", He meant the suffering He was about to endure. (Luke 22:42)

Could He have had similar feelings before coming to earth, knowing His fate? We can't know for sure, but we do know that He always wanted to do what His Father wanted Him to do.

Jesus said, "*For I have come down from heaven not to do My will, but to do the will of Him who sent Me.*" (John 6:38)

Sometimes we have to do things we don't like because they are part of a bigger plan that God has for us.

Do you ever feel afraid?
Lots of people do. Even Mary and Joseph felt afraid.

But when we know God, we don't need to be afraid because we trust in God who is greater than we are, who cares about us, and who can handle our concerns.

Maybe Mary and Joseph knew this verse from Psalm 56:3:
"When I am afraid, I put my trust in You."

When we feel afraid, we can ask God to help us, and He will. We will see our faith grow stronger when we trust Him.

Why were the angels so happy that Jesus was born?
Up until this point, the angels served as messengers. But their primary job is to worship God in heaven*. Now the Son of God they worshipped in heaven is wrapped in cloths and lying in a dirty, smelly manger.
*(Is. 6, Rev. 4 & 5)

And yet, Scripture tells us that a whole host of angels praised God. A host is like an army of angels. They were happy for us because they knew that God loves people and that Jesus came to bring us salvation.

How can you be like the angels, praising God, sharing the good news of His birth on earth?

How do you respond to hearing good news?
Do you keep it to yourself or share with others? What about the good news that God loves us and made a way for us to be part of His family?

Shepherds were not popular or respected people, but they were the first to hear the good news that Jesus was born and the only ones to see the whole company of angels. God loves everyone, even the ones who seem unimportant.

Like the shepherds, will you share the good news with others?

Later came the wise men who traveled from afar, always looking heavenward at the bright and shining star.

They brought some gifts and presents for the newborn King. They bowed down, full of joy, and worshipped Christ the King.

Why did the wise men bring gifts?
The wise men brought gifts as a way to worship Jesus and show they loved Him. The Bible names three gifts:
<u>Gold</u>: a gift for royalty, chosen for the King of the Jews, the King of Kings, who will one day rule over all the earth (Revelation 19:16)
<u>Frankincense</u>: a sweet smelling spice burned during sacrifices in the temple, a prediction of the death the Jesus would die as the sacrifice for the sins of all mankind. (1 Peter 1:18-19)
<u>Myrrh</u>: a spice that was used when someone was buried. When Jesus died, His body would be wrapped in linen with myrrh and aloes. (John 19:39-40)

The wise men's gifts were expensive, but they were happy to give them to Jesus. The Bible tells us that God loves it when we are generous and cheerful givers. (2 Cor. 9:6-7)

How can you be a generous and cheerful giver?

The baby's name was Jesus which means that He will save God's people from their sins, and He'd teach them to behave.

What does the name Jesus mean?
In Hebrew, the name Jesus is Yeshua, which means "he will save" or "savior." In Latin, it is Jesu. And in English, Jesu becomes Jesus.

Being our Savior was His primary mission, but in the 33 years that He lived on earth, Jesus taught us lessons, healed sick people, and did amazing miracles, all because He loves us.

How many other names for Jesus can you think of?

Why is the cross part of the Christmas story?
From the beginning, Jesus' plan was to live and to die for His people. *"The Son of Man came to serve and give His life as a ransom for many."* (Matthew 20:28)

Why did Jesus have to die? Someone had to be punished for all of our sins. Jesus offered to be punished instead of us. If we believe that and ask Him into our hearts instead of being punished for our sins, we'll live forever in a wonderful place call Heaven.

We can live forever because Jesus died in our place.

He was still a young man when
He died just like He said.
He saved us all while wearing
a crown of thorns upon His head.

But tears gave way to smiles
when the stone was rolled away.
He triumphed over death
on a glorious Easter day.

Why are we talking about Easter in the Christmas story?
The resurrection of Jesus the Christ is the cornerstone of the Christian faith and the culmination of the Christmas story. Jesus death was the reason He was born. It was a war between life and death. When Jesus arose from the grave He was the winner. That makes those who love Him winners too!

Jesus is in heaven now, but He sent His Spirit to guide us, His children, into all truth (Mark 16:19, John 1:12).

We have an invitation to heaven if we believe in Him and ask Him to live in our hearts.

What does it mean that can YOU be a shepherd or a wise man?
Jesus told Peter to feed His lambs – to take care of the people He loves. You can do that too. (John 21:15)

Listening to God makes us wise. You can be a wise man and show it by your good behavior and deeds done in wisdom (Psalm 119:98, Romans 16:19, James 3:13).

What can you do to be a shepherd or a wise man today?

How does God speak to you?
He spoke to Mary and Joseph through an angel. But today, He speaks to us in our hearts through the Holy Spirit. Jesus told His disciples, *"When the Spirit of truth comes, He will guide you into all truth. He will not speak on His own but will tell you what He has heard. He will tell you things to come."* (John16:13) And we have the same promise today. God speaks to us through His Spirit.

In order for us to hear from God, we must be listening.

Will you listen with all your heart?

Mythbusters

Mary and Joseph didn't travel alone.
Despite the multitude of Christmas cards depicting a dark silhouette of Joseph leading Mary astride a donkey on a lonely journey to Bethlehem, it is highly unlikely that they traveled alone. Any transit in those days was laden with danger so people traveled in groups or caravans.

Because Caesar Augustus decreed that a census be taken of the entire Roman world, "*everyone* *went to their own town to register*" (Luke 2:3). Therefore, many people would be en route in countless directions, including all Joseph's family and anyone from the line of David on their way to Bethlehem.

There is no mention of a donkey. Nor does it say that she gave birth the night she arrived in Bethlehem. Luke 2:6 simply says, "*while they were there, the time came for her to give birth.*"

There is no innkeeper.
Despite the multitude of Christmas pageants depicting a kindly or a harsh innkeeper, Scripture doesn't mention an innkeeper at all.

In those days, inns were lodgings with large or small rooms above a stable with stalls for the travelers' animals, which is the most likely place that Mary and Joseph settled in. The word for "inn" is also translated "upper room" so it's quite possible that they were on the ground floor of a family member's house.

Nor was Jesus born in a manger. Mary "*laid* Him in a manger", a feeding trough, normally along the wall of the stable underneath the rooms. "*And she gave birth to her firstborn son; and she wrapped Him in cloths, and laid Him in a manger, because there was no room for them in the inn.*" Luke 2:7

The Wise Men (Maji) weren't part of the "nativity."
Despite the images in nativity or manger scenes, the "*wise men from the east*" arrived much later than the shepherds. Scripture tells us that they went first to Jerusalem "*after Jesus was born in Bethlehem*" and met with King Herod, who then met with his priests & scribes before the maji went on their way. By the time the maji arrived to worship Jesus, there is no mention of a manger, He was called a child (not a baby), and His family was in a house (Matthew 2:1&11).

And despite images to the contrary, Scripture never refers to these men as kings or indicates they rode camels. Nor is there any mention of how many wise men there were; only three gifts are mentioned.

December 25 is not Jesus's birthday.

Despite all the Christmas season festivities in today's society, 2000 years ago, the scene was very different. Both the timing of a Roman census and shepherds being out in their fields at night indicate that it was highly unlikely that the event occurred in cold December.

While the gospel writers are very clear on the date and time of Jesus' death, there is no mention of the timing of His birth, and the early church didn't celebrate His birth at all. The Bible pays much more attention to Jesus' sacrifice and death, instructing us to commemorate it, but there are no directives to observe or honor His birth.

Over 300 years later, Emperor Constantine and/or Pope Julius 1 declared December 25 to be the official date, but no one today really knows why. One theory cites the transfer from a pagan celebration of the winter solstice and sun-worship to worship of the Son of Righteousness. Others dispute that. The more important point to remember is THAT He was born for us rather than WHEN He was born.

Thank you for taking time to read Mary Had A Little Lamb. If you enjoyed it, please consider telling your friends and posting a short review on Amazon and/or Goodreads. Word-of-mouth referrals are so appreciated.

For more on myths, talking points, Christmas traditions, recipes, free stuff, and tips to feel blessed, not stressed this holiday season, visit www.maryhadalittlelamb.net.

Susan Panzica is the author of *Mary Had A Little Lamb* and a contributor to three Chicken Soup For the Soul compilation books. Her passion is to bring an eternal perspective to earthly matters through writing, speaking, teaching, and coffee dates. Susan is a speaker, women and children's Bible teacher, and writer of the blog, Eternity Cafe, where she uses humble and hum-drum life experiences to highlight the holy.
www.susanpanzica.com

Susan is also an accidental abolitionist, the co-founder and Executive Director of Justice Network, which raises awareness about human trafficking, locally and globally.
www.justice-network.org

Zach Brose is the founder and lead designer of League Design Studio in Williamsburg, Brooklyn. He and his wife Tara share a passion for traveling, art, creativity and building the local church. Zach leads worship at Hillsong NYC, where he and his wife work with the creative team. He uses illustration, typography and design to bring life and imagination to ideas, brands, dreams and stories.
www.leaguedesign.us

Notes

Use this page to write down special dates, discussions, and memories with your child.